From Brokenness to Wholeness

-A Collection of stories of Faith, Adversity, Failures, Triumphs, & Forgiveness

Nadeen R. Cooper

Copyright

Dedication

This book is dedicated to my husband, Ricky A. Cooper, and my mother Sarah A. Hatchell. My husband is the person that has stood by my side through thick and thin. I can truly say that I have a man who is after God's heart, a man of true worship, a man who is humble, and a man who knows how to provide for his family. Yes he has been angry with me, but in the midst of it ALL he still loves me unconditionally and still comforts me in my hard times. I thank you Ricky for your faithfulness to God first and your family second. You rock as my husband and as our kid's father, but most of all as a MAN OF GOD. I love you!!!

My Mother has been my prayer warrior since I was born, we have had our differences but I can always say she is a woman of God and she will never turn her back on me or any of her girls. I am her baby and will always be her baby no matter how old I am, and she will always be my role model. I thank you for EVERY prayer you have ever lifted up to God on my behalf. I thank you Mother for your faithfulness to God first and your girls second. I love you! -Your baby girl Nadie.

Contents

Foreword by Ricky Cooper

I am proud to say that I have known the author of this book (Nadeen Cooper) for 20 years and have been married to her for 17 years. She is a person that is full of laughter, with a beautiful smile I might add, and a loving and caring heart for others. She enjoys puzzles, Lifetime Movie Network, watching Law and Order SVU, and listening to Gospel music. A mother of four, she definitely knows something about raising kids by herself and holding down the household when the government calls me on an assignment overseas.

Nadeen Cooper possesses the spiritual gift of evangelism and interpreting dreams. A true child of God, she loves to worship and dwell in the spirit of the Lord and obeys what the Lord says to her. She aspires to develop a program to help young teenage girls overcome the issues of life that happen to young girls during their teenage years. A true ambassador of the word of God and what God tells us to do and how to do it.

Foreword by Otescia Johnson

The book you are about to read was written by one of the most kind-hearted people I have ever had the honor of knowing. Nadeen has always been honest with me about who she is and what her intentions are. It's one of the things that drew me to her. She never tried to pretend she was perfect. She readily admitted her need for a Savior who could deliver her from her own internal struggles. Even more importantly, she showed me she was willing to be taught while simultaneously helping anyone at the drop of a dime, in any way she possibly could. Her smile lights up the room, and to be around her at her best is to witness true joy.

Nadeen and I met at a crucial time in both of our lives. She was working to develop her relationship with God and I was birthing a women's ministry. I never dreamed I'd have women in my home asking me all sorts of questions about the bible and how to walk with God, yet one phone call from Nadeen changed everything. That's just who she is. To really know her, is to know she has an innate ability to push you to be your best self… even when she doesn't realize she's doing it.

As you read Nadeen's book, I pray you hear her heart. Her greatest desire is to be a witness to the delivering power of God. She doesn't sugar coat her past, but she doesn't dwell there either. She is pressing toward the mark for the prize of the high calling of God in Christ Jesus (Philippians 3:14).

From Brokenness to Wholeness

-A Collection of stories of Faith, Adversity, Failures, Triumphs, & Forgiveness

Introduction

As you open this book and begin to read, I pray God gives you understanding of how a life can look and sound bad, yet have a beautiful ending. In this story, you will read some hurtful and shameful things that I have done to myself as well as my family.

I'll be the first to admit I'm not perfect. I've made mistakes that directly hurt the people who love me. On the other hand, I have also received some hurt from the people I love. Writing this book, I had to come to an understanding with God that there will be judgment. There will be people, who don't have a full understanding of our journey, who will chose to talk against my husband and me. We are prepared for what is to come, because we know once God has forgiven us, He doesn't hold anything over our heads. We are healed. Healed people do not hide in shame. They proclaim the goodness of the Lord who freely forgives us all. This assurance gives us the strength we need to share our story in hopes that others will be blessed. We understand that our story is not for our glory, but for God's glory only.

As you read this book, I pray for healing, wholeness, deliverance, peace, love and joy in your life. My goal of telling my story is to help the next person who is struggling with the issues of life that I had to struggle with. I realize all of my struggles were not for me alone. They were to equip me with the tools I would need to help someone else. With that in mind, I want to encourage you that life doesn't always have to be the way you see it now. There will be better days, just keep living!

I thank God for his strength for myself and my family. I thank God for every reader who will receive one of His many blessings from this book.

The Childhood

"I knew you before I formed you in your mother's womb. Before you were born I set you apart and appointed you as my prophet to the nations."
- Jeremiah 1:5

I was born in September of 1979 in Jacksonville, NC; the baby of four girls. My mother was a single parent who raised four beautiful girls, myself and my three sisters, who were the reason she chose the life she lived. My mother worked hard for her four girls, sometimes seven days a week just to make ends meet for our family. She else would. I always knew who my father was, but I barely saw him. He was in the military at the time I was conceived there in Jacksonville. My "Dad" would still come around every summer. He had a red car with the top down. But when I turned thirteen he seemed to have fallen off the face of the earth. I never saw him again, until later in life. That's when my mom decided to sit me down and tell me, the man I think is my father is not my father. I always wondered was that the truth or was it my mom's way of trying to protect me from the hurt of my father walking out of my life. So as the years went by I told myself that so I wouldn't hurt, knowing my mother was trying to protect me and not hurt me. As I got older I started to spend a lot of time in Richlands where my grandmother, and most of my aunts and

uncles lived. We always had family
gatherings where everyone would come over
to my grandmother's house to eat, laugh,
kids would play, and just have fun. My mom
never had a vehicle, so we would always
have to catch a ride there and back, which
was ok because we always had someone to
take us. We had a lot of family friends that
would stop and come through where my
grandmother lived on Petersburg Rd. At
that time, I began to develop in the body and
started looking more like I was a good
sixteen instead of thirteen, and we had this
one family friend who, as a man, did not
know how to keep his hands to himself. He
decided one Saturday when we were all over
there, to come over and do what he wanted
to me. He would always make little
comments here and there, but on that day he

18

found a way to get me around the house where no one was, and where no one could see us. He put his hands in places that should not have been touched by a grown man, or any man at that. After that incident, I tried everything I could not to go over to the family functions because I knew that family friend would always be there. But there were some days I couldn't avoid it, like birthdays and holidays. As a young girl I was always a quiet child who was happy in the house with her snacks, Care Bears, and cartoons. My mom didn't have to tell me to come inside too much, and while she worked and took care of the home, my older sister held down the house for our mom. So she really became my second mom instead of my big sister. She would make sure I had all my school work done, made sure I ate if our mom wasn't home, and made sure I had my bath and was ready for bed. But she would never take away from our mother's job as mom, because our mom did what she had to do in order for us to have what we needed.

My whole childhood I had a total of two friends, and they were my cousins, who I always felt a little less than. They were fortunate enough to have their mother and father in their life. So according to me, they had more than I did in life. I always compared myself to them, but I had one aunt tell me that I would never be like them. So that right there set my self-esteem to a very low point. After hearing that, I always thought I could do nothing better than them, or look better than them. One of my cousins' dad would take them out all the time, especially Christmas when he would take them shopping. That one cousin never looked down on me nor had anything ugly to say to me no matter how everyone else felt about me. Then one day the family got a call that our cousin's mom had passed away, so we all had to go over to my grandmother's house on the day of her mother's death. When I walked in the house, my cousin was the first person I saw, and right then she broke down in tears. At that moment, my best friend was hurting, and I didn't know what to do for her. In that broken time of my family's life, that's when that "family friend" made his next move on me. After that week I made up in my mind that I would not be going back over to my grandmother's house until that man disappeared. So now, not going anywhere on the weekends, I began to start branching out with other people around me and in school.

By this time, I was entering into my freshman year of high school and starting to interact with people from school and the neighborhood. Boys were starting to take interest in me, and I had my eye on a boy. Now I am fifteen, and this is where my life went from being the sweet little girl to the broken, unconfident, and violated teenager. Because one of the guys in the neighborhood decided he wanted me to be his girlfriend without my permission, I lost my virginity in a way that I never expected or wanted to. After that, I tried to avoid him to the best of my ability, but it was hard when he lived right upstairs above me. Then at sixteen I started dating the guy who would become my first son's father. I got pregnant at sixteen, and had my son Ray'quan at seventeen. When I had my son at seventeen, I was a junior in high school, and decided I didn't want to go back to school my 12th grade year. I began to work two jobs and take care of my son, and me and his father decided to go our separate ways. Now I had become that little girl my aunt had spoken over me. I had become that little girl with no education, no baby daddy, and just like my mother.

A Fatherless Daughter

"Father to the fatherless, defender of widows, this is God, whose dwelling is holy." -Psalms 68:5

As mentioned in Chapter 1, I was a fatherless daughter. As young girls we always desire the love and confirmation of our beauty from our father. Well I didn't have that from my biological father. I did get it from my sister's father who was there for my sisters and I, but there is nothing like hearing it from your own father... your own flesh and blood. Some days in the back of my head I would wonder why my father couldn't be around like my sisters' fathers. I had one sister whose father stayed in the house with us until his death. My older sister's father lived in Richlands where our family was from, even though she didn't spend as much time with him. I envied my other sister so much when it came to having a daddy because she was lucky enough to have two fathers who loved her. She had her biological father who stayed there in Richlands, and was lucky enough to have another guy who lived out of state to take care of her as well. As a little girl, what hurt the most, was watching the two cousins that are close in age with me be able to go spend the weekend with their dads and I couldn't. I did have a father however…a father who wanted to be there when it was convenient for him and not me. As a little girl, I remember him coming to visit for the summer and him pulling up in his red car with the top down. He would take me out and I would have lots of fun. Spending time with him made me feel like everyone else… I have a daddy. Then somehow, that all faded away. I don't know what happened, but all I remember is I didn't have a daddy anymore. So at thirteen as I'm getting older, I start to question my mom, and I remember one day she sat me down in her room. She was walking around doing something in the room and I had sat down in a small chair. I can still hear it like she is saying it to me right now.

"Nadie it's time for you to know the truth. Ray really isn't your daddy. Your daddy is a guy named Robert Wells from South Carolina."

I remember crying and wondering, "W*hy now? Why is she telling me this? I don't even know a Robert!"*

Time went by and I still never heard anything from Ray or saw him. At this point, I don't even know if he is alive or dead. So, I just went on with life the best way I could as a child, but still with a lot of questions in my head. When someone walks out of your life and gives you no answers, you tend to wonder,

"What's wrong with me, why did they have to leave me?"

Well, me being me, I still love that man just as if I saw him every day, and just like he never left. You have to know I had some questions in my mind about my mom telling me this.

I wondered, "*Did she tell me this to shut me up about not having my dad? Is she telling me this because she doesn't know herself? Is this even the truth?*"

My momma was and still is my world. I never doubted anything she did for us. So, it wasn't hard for me to forgive my mom for telling me that, but I still wondered *why* she told me that. I thought maybe she was telling me that because she didn't want me to hurt anymore, but sometimes a mother's love for her children will make her blind. Her telling me that hurt me even more, but as I grew older and understood life more, I knew her intentions were good toward me.

At age sixteen I got pregnant with my first son and wanted my father to be a part of our lives so bad that I gave my son his name, RAY. I thought one day I would be able to talk with him and he'd get to meet my son. That still hasn't happened to this day. So as life goes on, I continue to do what the "typical girl" does when she doesn't have her father in her life. I looked for the love from guys who turned out to be no good for me. I always found guys who "loved me" but didn't know how to keep their hands to themselves, or chose to talk to me like I was nothing.

Then on Mother's Day, May 10, 2009, I got an unexpected phone call from my father, asking me how I was doing. I had so many emotions, I didn't know whether to be happy, sad, or angry, but I went on with the conversation with him. And for the last eight years, I have gone through a lot of emotions with the man I call Daddy. The first year or two, we would communicate back and forth, send each other gifts for birthdays, Christmas, kids' birthdays, etc. He would make plans to come to Georgia to see me and my family, and he even went as far as inviting us to his family reunion one year. Then he got sick, and had to have open heart surgery. In the process of him having open heart surgery, I had two people contact me. One of his friends contacted me asking how my "father" was doing. That was a big question to me, because that let me know he was talking about me with others and referring to me as his "daughter". When he would talk with me he would always refer to me as *sweetie*, or his *baby girl.* There were times his sisters would contact me on social media and refer to me as their niece, so another sign that I was being talked about to others as his daughter. So during his heart surgery, my second contact from someone on his end was his daughter, my sister. She called me, and I picked up the phone.

"Hello."

I hear, "Hello. My name is Latrice, and my father Racine left your number for me to update you on his surgery."

I said, "Oh ok! Well, how is he doing?"

She let me know he was doing well, and I am on the other end thinking, "*WOW! She really don't know who I am."* So, I asked her, "Well did he tell you who I was?"

She says, "No I just assumed you were a good friend."

I said, "Well baby, I am not just a friend. I am his daughter!"

Her response was, "You're his daughter?!"

"Yes, his daughter!" I said.

"Well are you from here in Chicago, and how old are you?" she asked.

"No, I am from North Carolina, and I am 36 years old," I told her.

I already knew about her and knew she was one year younger than me, so we went on with our conversation. I shared some of my life and she shared some of hers. Well, that didn't last long, because a couple weeks later, I didn't hear from him or his daughter. I guess he wasn't ready or prepared for his other children to know about me. Months went by. I would call to check on him and see how everything was going with his health, but one day I decided to message him and let him know how I was feeling as a fatherless daughter. Instead of him responding to my email, his new wife, whom I never met, decided to respond. She goes on telling me that Ray is not my father, and I will not have anything to do with him. She said he was a great father and grandfather to the kids around him now. She continued with, "He said he don't even know who you are, and he's never seen you before."

That was so heart breaking and funny at the same time, because this man has pictures of me, my kids, and MY MOTHER on his social media page, but here is his wife saying he doesn't know me. So, I left it alone that night, but when I did pull my emotions back together I wrote him a nice letter letting him know he will always be my father in my eyes. I pray one day before we leave this earth he will come to recognize me as his daughter.

Knowing I am being **talked about** as his daughter, but not being **acknowledged** as his daughter, compounded the other issues I already had. Remember, I grew up without a father in my life, and I was mistreated by guys. The experienced with my Dad caused my already low self-esteem to drop even more.

After the heartache of my youth and becoming a single mom, I'd started to believe I wasn't worthy of having a man in my life. I thought I wasn't good enough for anyone to love me. BUT GOD had other plans. He sent me an angel straight from Heaven in 1998, but didn't realize I had him until 2009. We'll talk more about him later!

The Alcohol Addiction

"The temptations in your life are no different from what others experience. And God is faithful. He will not allow the temptation to be more than you can stand. When you are tempted, he will show you a way out so that you can endure". 1 Corinthians 10:13

The first time I moved away from home, my family, and everything I knew, was in September 2001. I had just gotten married the year before. My husband joined the military to make a better life for our family. I had two kids, and was pregnant with my third child when we got to Washington state many miles away, across the country, away from everyone I knew. The war in Afghanistan had just begun after the attack on America in September 2001. That meant my husband was about to be sent off to another country. So now here I am, so far away from family or anyone that I know, with two children and pregnant with another, and my husband's about to be leaving for a year. I had my third child in May of 2002 and everything was going good. I had to grow up FAST. I had to learn how to be a mother and a wife while standing on my own two feet. Before that, I always had our families back home to help me with the children. I always had a job, and knew how to work and take care of us all. But now everything was different. I was a house wife and a mother of three. So, life in Washington state keeps going, and I began getting home sick here and there. I would start having one glass of wine to take the edge off.

After a few years, I became pregnant with my last child. Right after finding out I was pregnant, my husband got orders to go to war, again. He left in April 2004 and returned home for two weeks when I had my baby in August 2004. When he left to go back overseas life began to get hard. As a result, my drinking got heavier and heavier. It got to the point where every day I had to have my fried fish, beer, and fries for lunch while I watched my soaps. Sounds so depressing huh? So that means I was picking

up my kids from school under the influence.
I used to tell myself,

*"Well at least I'm walking to get them and not
driving."*

My addiction to alcohol had become very
heavy. Alcohol addictions usually come with
other habits that are not appealing to God or
your life. I started to hang out with other
wives who drank and partied. One thing
about a person with an addiction, they will
start to make excuses for everything to make
themselves look good. In becoming an
alcoholic, now I couldn't help but to think,

*"You have become a nobody. You have become that
woman people have said you would become. You're
nothing but a drunk now, with four kids and a
husband who is never around."*

At that point, I had to have a drink every night to go to bed. When you begin to drink every day and every night, there are some things that come with it, like infidelity. So, I began to cheat on my husband and of course cheaters have to lie. Cheating and lying go hand in hand. At this point, my husband is still deployed so he doesn't know what's going on back home. When he returned home, I was that wife who was outside from the time the kids went to school until the time the husbands came home from work. I would make sure the house was clean, and dinner was done so by the time he got home from work I was ready to go out. In the process of picking up the drinking habit, I also picked up the habit of gambling. The post I lived on had a bowling alley with slot machines in it, and that is where I would be every night. I would go with money and come back with no money, which was not good for my family. Not only was I losing money in my addiction of drinking, but now I am losing it in my addiction of gambling. There were many days we struggled financially, but I was too selfish to see how I was hurting my family.

In 2005 our whole unit came down with orders to move to Germany, and I began thinking, this could be a new beginning for us. I would finally be getting away from the things and people that are not helping my family right now. But you know what? We can't blame others for our issues. We have to learn to face ourselves in the mirror. But if you don't take the time to fix you, that same YOU will be going to your next destination.

That's exactly what happened. I was excited about the move but wasn't too excited to fix "me" before going to Germany.

When we got to Germany and got settled in, everything was going great. Then once again like always, life hit us. We have to learn to handle life the way God wants us to handle life, not the way we want to handle life. But before I knew that information, I handled life the way Nadeen would handle life, and that was through drinking. So there we were in Germany, the Land of Alcohol, where they have this thing called "Oktoberfest". During Oktoberfest, they celebrate by drinking alcohol. Lots and lots of alcohol! Oh yeah, I was so ready! But I wasn't ready for the heartache that was coming behind my drinking. At that stage of my life, I had to have something to drink at all times. One night, I had gotten so drunk, all I remember was falling in the parking lot of my neighborhood, then becoming sick all over my bedroom and bathroom. The next morning when I awoke I remembered thinking to myself,

"Where are those "friends" that helped me get drunk?"

You would have thought that was it for me, and that would be the end of my drinking journey. Who wants friends that's going to drink with you, but leave you in the parking lot laid out and drunk? Well nope that wasn't it! I wasn't done until New Year's Eve night in 2008. As we prepared to go into 2009, we had a Black & White party. Three of us ladies decided we wanted to start our New

Year right, so we made a pact to go to church.

On January 4, 2009, we decided we were going to go to church, and we are going to serve God with no turning back. But as of that moment, I still hadn't given up drinking. The night before we're supposed to start going to church, I did what I did and that's drink and get drunk. The morning for church came, and everyone was ready to go, but I was hungover, so I was sooooo not ready! But in the spirit realm, I was to ready to go. Because one thing about me, I knew who Jesus was, but I just didn't have that relationship with Him. Nevertheless, we went to church and instantly I was hit by the Spirit of God. Right then I asked God to remove the taste of alcohol from me and

44

take my desire away of wanting it. All Glory be to God! I was delivered from all my alcohol taste and addiction on that day. Once again, God had given me the way out of an addiction that was taking over my life and my family's life.

The Abusive Man

Years later after my family has relocated back to the States, I was working at my station on my job, when I was approached by this guy that found interest in me. When he approached me, he was looking for someone to vent to. As he went on about the current problem he was having, I listened and gave advice. In my mind, this would not go any further than just talking. But the next thing I knew, on November 2nd he was asking me to lunch. Once again, I am thinking, *lunch…sure! Nothing to that!*

Everything will be ok. Well we ended up going to lunch on that day. As we sat and ate lunch, he began to pour out to me about life. He told me how he was married to a woman, but they don't even talk, and he has papers at the house to file for divorce. He lives with another woman he has been with for five years, but they are on the verge of breaking up because she is controlling, nosey and always arguing with him. I know what you're thinking,

"Girl what in the world were you doing?"

As a married woman I thought, *this can't hurt anything. I'm just having lunch. That's it!* My husband was deployed at the time, and I should have known better, because me knowing what my issues are, I know I get lonely. All it took for the enemy was for me to open that crack in the door for the ole snake to slide on in. Well, as we sat and talked, he began to tell me things I haven't heard in some months now, like *you're so beautiful, you're so wise, you're so intelligent…* the enemy even knows how to encourage you too. So later that day, he asked if I could give him a ride home and I said, "Sure!" As we approached his home, he invited me in to see it, being it was a newly built home. We went inside, and he starts to show me all around the home from bedroom to bedroom. He told me who slept where, BUT he didn't tell me where he slept. So, me being me at the time, I looked at him and said, "So if she sleeps here, and your roommate sleeps there, where do you sleep? Because I know if you're staying here with a woman, you must be sleeping with her, and

48

there must be a relationship." He went on to tell me that most nights he sleeps on the couch, or he will sleep at the foot of the bed. As we are standing in the kitchen of another woman's house, he steps into me, embracing me, and kisses me. Right then I knew, *uh oh. This is not good.* Well, this is where the lies start, and I should have run then, but NOPE! I didn't.

After that day, I became his ride to work. Man! Why in the world did I choose to do that? After that, breakfast dates, lunch dates, etc. became more and more frequent. On November 4th he invited me over to hang out with him and his friends from the "subdivision". I was planning on going over and hanging out, but couldn't make it. I didn't hear anything from him for a couple of hours. Around midnight, I get a call asking can I come pick him up because "the lady" he lives with and her friend, the roommate, have started an argument with him and he feels it's going to get bad. He said he just needed to get to a hotel, so things didn't get out of control. I wasn't able to pick him up due to having to pick my son up from a football game. The next thing I knew, he was calling me telling me that a neighbor is bringing him to a hotel in the town where I lived.

That night he texted me all night talking about how he needs to see me, he needs to be with me, he needs me in his life, etc. I had to take him to work the next day, so I told him I would see him in the morning. Here comes my biggest mistake besides giving him a ride. I decided to go to his room at 5am that morning, but we didn't have to leave until 6am. So when I got to the room, he insisted I lay down with him since we had an hour left. I laid down with him, he started to massage my body, began kissing on me, and one thing led to something else. The morning went on and I took him to work and picked him up. After he got off, I took him home, scared for him, thinking he was going back into a danger zone with the ladies. Then the following weekend, November 11th, we had his birthday. I wanted him to have a great birthday. I got us a room in one of the finest hotels in town on that Friday night. We ate dinner and just enjoyed each other's company. Then, as usual, I took him back home the next morning and he went out with friends on that day to celebrate his birthday. The next day, I met his son for the first time.

He's asked me if I could come take his son home. I agreed, and we left to take his son home. Instantly I loved his son. He had a great sense of humor and we shared great laughter together. When we dropped his son off, it wasn't his home. It was his son's grandparent's home; this man's mom and dad's house. I said, "You're not going to go speak to your parents?" And that's when we had our very first disagreement. He told me, "Nope! I don't talk with either one of them and I will not discuss this." This was another RED FLAG! I should have run because my mother always said,

"the way a man treats his mother will be how he treats his woman."

As the months went on we just enjoyed each other and got to know each other even more. As we approached the end of the year, we began to talk more about how we can't continue to be together as long as he is living with another woman, even though I am still married. He started talking about moving out and me being a "fool in lust" because it wasn't love if he wasn't my husband. I began to tell him I would help him move whenever he was ready. The relationship between us couldn't continue to go on, as long as he was in that house because, according to him, the arguments were getting worse by the day.

On November 25th he got real sick and I had to take him to the hospital. I've never seen a man so sick. Not even my husband. I was so scared for him. That was the day I learned who his wife was. When we arrived at the hospital they started asking him about his emergency contact information. When it came down to his Wife.......his response was, "I don't even know her phone number." That was also the day his mother came up again. I asked him if he had to have surgery or anything, should I go get his mother. He told me, "NO you just stay by my side." This was yet another RED FLAG to run......But I didn't run! I did just as he asked and stayed by his side.

I got a hotel room, so he could rest and take his medicine the right way. That Sunday we decided to go down to Jacksonville, and on the way back he took me to meet a friend. The friend I met was like no friend I'd ever meet in my whole life. A couple of days later he made the decision to move in with that friend, so one evening after work we went and sat with the friend and agreed on bills and terms of the living arrangement. On December 3rd he moved out of the "subdivision" and into his friend's home. So now he lives less than 5 minutes from me and we can see each other and spend time together as much as we wanted. Now that all of this had happened, how was life going to be on my end at home? Well, as we grew closer and closer I became very distant from my home, family, and church home. He would be the gentleman any woman could ask for, at least until he got you where he wanted you. He would showcase me to the people at work, his one friend at the time, cook for us every day, and made sure I never wanted for anything.

Our first blow up argument was Christmas Eve. His friend had left out of town for the holiday and I had made plans for him and I to spend Christmas Eve together. Well Christmas Eve came and he decided he needed to go "help a friend's wife" put furniture together, and that took all day. When he finally got back to me it was a huge argument. One thing I've learned in life is that people will make time for who they want to make time for. That was one thing we always fought about; him spending time with everyone except me. I used to tell him you showboat me in front of the work place and outside the home, but behind closed doors that was a different story.

One day in January as I arrived at his home, his friend ran out to the car to let me know he had been sitting with him drinking and "crying" about life. And here is the good old caring Nadeen… Being me, I run in because him crying is unusual, but also that fake charm. He had shared stories about his life, and him growing up, and how he talked with his grandmother and how she always knew how to read him and touch his heart. Well this is where things went left for him instead of right. He gave me his grandmother's phone number, so I could talk with her. All he wanted was the "love of his life" to speak with his grandmother. On the way home that evening I decided to call her, but it was not the call he or I had expected to hear. When I get on the phone with his grandmother, she began to tell me, "Baby you sound like a very sweet girl and I don't want you to get hurt." RED FLAG!! She goes on to say, "You better not put nothing in your name, and if I was you I would RUN for my life!" ANOTHER RED FLAG!!! She then asked me if I knew about his background, and if I was willing to live with that lifestyle.

Lord God, why in the world did I not listen to that woman? Let me tell you why! It was because I was 'in lust". I went back and told him the call didn't go as you planned, and that his grandmother told me to run for my life… After that, he cut his grandmother off! We got through the New Year as a "couple", and the apartment next door to our friend came open so he talked to the landlord about getting that apartment. One thing about this man, he was one sweet talker, and he could get anything he wanted once he put his mind to it as long as he put on that fake charm. He moved into the house next door. Now one thing I did do was keep that sweet grandmother's voice in the back of my head, so nothing was put in my name. But I didn't let the "love of lust" go. Shame on me, because I furnished the WHOLE house from the bedroom right down to the forks and spoons.

In March, my husband came back home from overseas and I let him know I had gotten involved with another man and I would be moving out. The time came, and I moved in with this man. That's where it all begins, the "woman's place". One thing about me, I am not a soft-spoken person, but instead a very loud out spoken woman. I never hold back on how I feel, never sugar coat anything, never speak negative to anyone nor do I allow them to speak it to me. All that changed in just one months' time frame. This man went from cooking every day and words of encouragement, to expecting HIS meal to be done at a certain time and belittling me. I went from the sweetest, loving, and best person in the world, to a controlling, negative, nosey, and loud mouth, not knowing my place, type of woman. I remember one night we were laying in the bed talking and he looked at me and said,

"You need to learn to shut the f*** up sometimes, you talk too d*** much!"

That was the very first time I had ever had anyone tell me that I talked too much. I know my purpose here on Earth. I know the reason God created me; it is to speak and spread the gospel to nations, from state to state. And now I have let this man come into my life and snatch that knowledge away from me......SHAME ON ME! When he spoke that over me it did something to me. As the months went by, I became less confident in myself. I went from smiling to crying day in and day out. I began walking on egg shells thinking I was going to say or do something wrong. He would even tell me I had mental issues.

One night he decided he wanted to leave at 8'oclock pm and come back at like 2'oclock am and wanted me to be ok with that. That was the very first time he had done that, but not the last time. It started to be a routine, especially on Friday nights when he would get paid. Then it became a habit of coming in and getting sex how he wanted it in any manner. It got to the point where on Wednesday or Thursday he would start an argument with me just, so I could be mad on Friday. I guess in his head if I was mad he didn't have to stay around. When we would argue he would not talk to me for 3 to 5 days at a time. He would be in the house with me and wouldn't say one word to me. He would expect me to still be in my "woman's place" and do the things a woman was expected to do, like cook, clean, and cater to him even though he was not speaking to me. As we would have our days of not talking, I would sit there and cry and wonder,

"Why are you here Nadeen, this is not you? This is not who you were born to be, and this is not the life God has called you to be in."

We took a trip to Florida with our neighbor to see his family and have Easter with them. When we got there the family was super nice to us and made us feel so welcomed. He kept telling everyone I was a pastor and I preach the word. He would have so many nice things to say about me. The next morning, we went to church with the family, having a normal Easter just as if we were husband and wife, but the only thing was, I was missing my family, especially my kids. Later that day as some prepared for dinner, I did family photos for our friend and his family. In the process we also took "family" photos. After that we went out on a walk in the park and took more pictures, just him and I. As we walked I looked at him and I said, "Larry, I really enjoyed this, but I am not happy because what we are doing is sin. So as long as we are in this together, still married, neglecting family, this is never going to work."

Months and months continue to go by. The lack of attention was heavy, and the name calling became worse. I would struggle with staying there and being back home with my family, the ones who truly loved me, really missed me, and wanted me home. I was there for this man. He never had to want for anything, nor did his kids. I was there when his first grandchild was born. I was even in the delivery room where I was given the name GiGi. And all he could do was talk down to me and tell me I had mental issues. I was so blinded by the lust and stronghold, I began to live the life that was not me at all, and the life God did not give me to live. There were days I would pray, *"Lord please bring a woman his way to take him from me. Lord please give him the strength to tell me to leave."* This became my prayer. Well that day came, and it hurt so bad, but I kept telling myself, *you prayed for this!* But the knowledge that I have in the Lord could have prevented me from the pain if I would have just followed His instructions. The Lord says, "Adultery is a sin", and we all know sin brings pain. We all know there is "Consequences to our Curiosity".

One year after this man walked up to me at work, he pushed me away like I was a piece of trash on the street. This man had an agenda and he needed it to be filled. He moved back in with the woman who was so-called "controlling, nosey, and evil". In the process of him moving back in with her, he then moved his daughter, her boyfriend, and their baby into the house we built together; the house I bought EVERYTHING for. Through this whole trial that I brought upon myself, I learned that you should never let anyone change who you are in Christ and make you become a person to their liking.

The wrong person makes you beg for attention, affection, commitment, and love. The right person gives you these things because they truly love you. Withholding affection is psychological manipulation, and abuse is NOT LOVE!

The Faithful Husband

"At last!" the man exclaimed. "This one is bone from my bone, and flesh from my flesh! She will be called 'woman, because she was taken from 'man." -Genesis 2:23

I met my husband on January 13, 1998. I started working with my cousin at Taco Bell where the both of them worked. When I started this job, I was a single mother, and this was my second job. When I walked in I asked my cousin if there were any guys that worked there. Her response, "Nobody but him." I said, "Oh no!" not knowing that was my angel sent from heaven at the time. So as time goes by he starts to flirt with me, but my life at the time was so caught up in the "Thug Life" guys; guys that thought I wasn't worth loving, just worthy enough to lay down with. I was also working two jobs trying to take care of my son, and really wasn't looking for love, or a guy to be with. At the same time, I was not happy with life either because I had become that young girl that everyone said I would be......the dropout with a baby and no baby daddy. God had other plans for me though. I am so glad I have grown to know we don't have to go off of what people say about us, but what God has to say about us. Every day he would ask me when I was going to let him come see my baby. Everyone knew that was his excuse to get close to me. Well let me tell

68

you, it wasn't an excuse with him. He really wanted to see my son and love his mother at the same time.

One day he called and asked if there was anything I needed. I thought to myself, *"Don't no dude just call you and ask if there's anything you need. He must want something in return."*

Well let me tell you again... NOPE! He didn't want anything but my time! That was it! I tried and tried to find something wrong with this guy, because I was just used to those who wanted nothing from me but sex, or to take care of them. I even went so far as to avoiding sexual contact with him just to see if he would leave me alone, and NOPE! It didn't work! Instead, he started hanging out with me and my family more and more.

69

When my son turned a year old, he was right there for him just like he was his own. He even went as far as paying for the whole birthday celebration! Shortly after that we started doing things like a family, but in the midst of it all, I was still caught up on the external interests that were no good for me.

In June of 1999, I found out I was pregnant with my second child and my now husband had gone back to school to finish his last year of college. He would come home on the weekends to see us, or I would go up to where he was to spend the weekend with him. One evening in February of 2000, he came over to the house to take me out, but before we left he asked could he speak with my mom. At the time, both my mom and sister were there, and he spoke with both of them to ask if he could marry me. So that night he took me out to Freedom Jewelers and told me to pick a ring, and he asked me right there in the store to be his wife. I said YES of course, but unfortunately, I didn't love him the way he loved me. I was thinking to myself,

"I am pregnant for the second time, and I am really becoming that girl people say I am."

It didn't even matter that the father was there. In March 2000 we had our first child together, and I knew he was going to be a great father because he already was to my son. On August 5, 2000 we got married, and became one. That was a very emotional but exciting day. That day I had experienced rejection and rejoicing within the same hours. Even though we had a church wedding we only had about ten people there to support us, and sadly, he had no family there. At the time of our marriage his father nor his family approved of our relationship, because to them I was just a young girl with a son and about to tear their young son's life apart. Even though we had been together for two years by that time, I had been holding my end up on a job, had my own place, and he had graduated from college, people still saw me as the girl who would tear his life apart. I faced rejection from his family, and what was so bad was that I also had to face rejection from my family as well. As always my family would pick and choose who they celebrated. The same weekend of my wedding I had a cousin whose son turned a year old, and the family instead decided that it would be best to go celebrate his birthday.

I had to have a guy from church to walk me down the aisle because I could not find my dad anywhere or get ahold of him. So now the wedding is over, and we are back to our life, but this time as husband, wife, mother and father. Even though he had just graduated from college, he could not find work in his field, so he had to make a decision, and it was one that would change our life as a family. In October 2000 he decided to join the military. When he joined the military to make a better life for us, I instantly went into a lonely state of mind. That's when the adultery began. When he left for boot camp I went back to dating a guy I had dated before. This guy had moved in with me, was driving my car around town, and everything. My husband was in boot camp and I was carrying on life like I wasn't even married. Months go by and my mother begins to notice what I have going on and does not approve of it; so that destroyed our relationship as mother and daughter. We stayed less than a minute away from one another and did not talk because of the situation. After my husband graduated Boot Camp and AIT, it was time for us to relocate to our first duty station. We were sent to Washington State, miles and miles away from home and our family. When we arrived to our first duty station I found out that I was pregnant, and knowing that I had been unfaithful to my husband, I wondered if my baby was my husband's baby or the guy that I had been dating. So my mom came to visit us after I had my son and she tells me either I could tell my husband, or she would. Only three people knew this baby may not have been my husband's; my cousin, my mom and the "other" guy. I am sure others thought the same because I didn't hide what I was doing, but one thing about my husband was, even if he knew, he wouldn't say anything to me because I truly believe he tried to see the best in me.

The night had come for me to tell him about the baby, so we went out on a date. As we went out and enjoyed ourselves I was thinking to myself, "*If I tell this man that the baby we just had may not be his, I'm going to die.*" We had gone to one of the river fronts on our date, and I just knew that he would drown me right there. So here it was. I looked my husband in the eyes and said, "Ricky, our baby Dariuse might not be yours." The first time I had ever seen my husband cry, other than over his mother's death, was that night in that moment. He looked at me and said, "Baby, it's ok. That is my son and will always be my son." I told him that if he wanted, we could get a DNA test done, but he looked at me again with so much pain in his eyes and said to me, "NO we will not get a test done because that is my son." He made it clear that he didn't want to talk about it anymore and he would deal with it later in the future if we had to.

I thank God for his Grace and Mercy over our life, and for the creation of genes because as our son grew older, the more and more he began to look like my husband, his father. After that night we moved forward with life as a family. He was a man of courage, faith, and lots of love. He loved me

From Brokenness to Wholeness

like I was the only woman on earth, NEVER told me no to anything, always worked, and provided for me and the kids. We never had to want for anything as a family. He would always make sure we had any and everything we ever needed. So, in 2006 we received orders to move to Germany, and I said to myself, *Well Lord, hopefully this journey will be better than the last one.* Even though I didn't walk with the Lord didn't mean I didn't know the Lord. When I was 17 I gave my life to God, so I knew God and what my calling was over my life. I just let this thing called life control me more than Jesus, and when you give your life to God, but don't surrender to God, you still have given the enemy room to come in.

77

When we moved to Germany I wanted to surrender to God but I hadn't completely done that yet. When I got to Germany my husband deployed a year later, and there I was again feeling lonely in my pity parties. I had a group of friends that would see the God in me but wouldn't help pull the God out of me. I found myself caught up in so much drama, and so much mess. My drinking picked up and I was hanging out and partying more and more. Once again, I found that no good friend, at least not good for me, and he was so full of charm and sweet talk. I always wondered, *"Nadie, why do you allow the sweet talkers to suck you in?"* It was always the same pattern! The guys that only wanted sex, money, and anything else they could suck out of you. It had to be something within myself that was drawn to this. Could it be I wanted love or attention that bad? What was wrong with me, and why did I feel like I needed to find love somewhere else when I had all the love I could ask for at home? Well when I got involved with this new man, I got more than I could bargain for. He didn't love me! All he wanted was that one thing. Sex... He was also married, and his wife was deployed as well. With him, I ended up pregnant and decided to go back home to the States that summer and made a decision I thought I would never make in my life. I decided to have an abortion. And because of the shame and embarrassment when I went back to Germany, I began to lie to people about what really happened. I told some the baby died, while I told others that I had given the baby up for adoption. But we all know once you start lying you have to keep up with your lies, and sometimes that can be hard.

I had some friends that began questioning my story, but I couldn't begin to tell the truth when I couldn't even deal with the truth myself. So as time passed, I became somewhat healed from that situation, which I didn't think you ever could. But when it came to me doing wrong I couldn't hold it in; I always had to open my mouth and tell someone. So even though I was still coming to terms with it myself, I opened up. Sometimes, opening my mouth was more trouble than the trouble I was already in. That's what had happened here in this situation. I decided to tell a "friend" who decided to tell other "friends" and yeah, so then everyone was looking at me sideways. I couldn't be mad though right? I did this to myself and put myself out there right? I now had to face a different dilemma. I was sitting there like,

"I have to tell my husband because if not someone else will."

I decided to tell my husband, and he was not happy. Do you blame him for being upset? I don't. But here I am acting up again and doing stuff a wife should not be doing. This time my husband was really tired of it, and he demanded I get myself together, become the wife I was called to be, or he would be divorcing me. At that point I knew I had to make a change. Not just for myself, but for my family, because I was about to blow the whole thing.

In January 2009, I decided to really submit to God and resist the Devil... BUT we all know when you do that the enemy becomes angry. Yes, the Bible tells us that the Devil will flee if we submit to God, BUT the Bible ALSO says,

No weapon formed against us will prosper, and every tongue will be condemned that comes against you.

In that verse, God says the weapon WILL NOT prosper, but He didn't say it wouldn't form. When I decided to walk for Jesus, the weapons formed and the tongues started moving. But I won't sit here and act like I had no part in those tongues and weapons because the Bible also says you will REAP WHAT YOU SOW. I had some bad soil that God needed to clean up, and when it's clean up time with God, He will allow some things to happen in order for you to be cleaned up. So that year I lost all of my friends, went through some sickness, and had lots of hurt and pain. My husband and I needed healing, so God let some things happen to get us to that healing place. Later in the months, we got orders that took us back to the States. We were set to move to Georgia, and at this point I was walking with the Lord, got my head straight and was praying that God be a fence around me please! We arrived in Georgia in August of 2009, and my husband once again leaves on another deployment in 2010. I am saying to myself and pleading, *"HEY GOD PLEASE BE A FENCE"!!* To God be the Glory, He was my fence through that deployment. He gave me and the kids a church home while Ricky was deployed, and when he came back, everything was good. He joined us at church and got involved in ministries there. I was working at the church, one of the leaders in the church, and everything was good.

Then 2013 hit, and my husband was deployed again… *"Lord be a fence!"* This time the kids were older, and things began to get a little crazy again. My oldest son started to get involved in things he shouldn't have and started hanging with people he shouldn't have been with. The Lord started speaking with me about things that would take me out of my comfort zone. And we all know no one wants to come out of their comfort zone, right? So, I started acting like Jonah in the whale's belly, being disobedient to the Lord's word. When that starts happening, a

WHOLE lot of things start moving, but not in your favor. So, I started to have those pity parties again, the rejection of myself started again, loneliness started again, all the enemy targets started coming again because he knew I wasn't suited and booted like I should have been in the Lord. Shame on me! I became depressed, sad, and somewhat crazy… I stopped going to church, quit my job at the church, and just started letting the devil use me like a fool. One evening I was so tired of life I decided that would be the night I would make everything ok and end my own life. BUT THE DEVIL IS A LIE because in the midst of my depression and crazy thoughts God was working behind the scene.

You're probably wondering HOW He was working because you KNOW it was something big, because I am still HERE! Well, as I sat on my couch with the bottles of pills in my hand ready to overdose on everything I had, my phone rang. My niece called to tell me that my great niece was having a seizure and the ambulance was on the way to get her. Even in it all God will use another tragedy to pull you out of your mess and in the end, me and my baby girl (my great niece) were both ok.

But in the midst of it all I didn't forget who Jesus was. I did however, forget to let Him live in my heart. So, there I was bringing heartache to my husband again. He was overseas with the worries of living through each day, and back home his wife can't even hold it together. So, God allowed me to fall, but He kept me because that's the kind of God we serve. That's when I also learned God has to break you in order to build you back up. He allows things to happen in our life that are not normal for us. But once I got tired He put me in a place with Him that helped me depend on Him instead of the people around me.

By the time my husband returned home, we were able to grow closer in the Lord together. His family was in church again, and he was able to come home and step right into his calling. For everything we went through as a family, God gets all the glory. Some may look at us and say that most of the things we went through came from my own sinful ways, but the God we serve will pick us up from out of our pit, forgive us, clean us up and push us right into our destiny. That pit doesn't always mean sin, it could be depression, loneliness, anger, etc. But always remember when God cleans us up and forgives us, He puts it in the sea of forgetfulness, and He will never bring it back up or hang it over our head. Because of all our trials, hurt, pain and shame we can really lift our heads and live the blessed life.

Living My Best Life

-Don't walk away from your connection!

So now that you have heard my story of brokenness, now let me tell you how I became whole again. In the midst of the hurt, pain, shame and rejections you can still come out shining bright with Gods glory. Only God can forgive you for all the things you have done wrong, help you to raise four beautiful kids without destruction, and allow you to keep a great husband. One thing about God is He knows when you are broken, and He knows when you are not ready to be whole in Him. But in the midst of it all, He will still protect you, watch over you, and not allow too much damage to be done in your life.

As a little girl I grew up with many doubts toward myself, a lot of rejection from people which turned into rejection towards myself. Now that I have grown older and wiser, I have realized that when I start to reject myself, I also reject God. When I doubt myself, I also doubt God. Living the life I have lived up to this point, I have carried a lot of rejection, pain and shame towards myself. Because in my head, I am saying surely God if I have done so bad in my life, have been mistreated, have been rejected from people... How am I supposed to tell anyone the good about me?

So, here I am in year 2018. I'm beginning to live the blessed life. I have released my first book (thank you for your reading), but now YOU may be wondering how am I able to do that after the life I have lived? You may be asking, after all the years of bringing hurt, pain and shame to my husband and kids... How are you able to live a blessed life? I'm so excited you asked!

I am able to live a blessed life because I serve a BIG GOD! I serve a God who forgives. I serve a God who will turn my trouble into HIS story for HIS glory! I am able to be the wife, mother, friend, manager, writer, minister, and everything else God has called me to be. Right now… I am about to sit by my husband's side and help him minister to people who are broken and want to be whole in God. We are able to sit side by side and counsel other married couples who are going through the same pain and brokenness my husband and I have gone through. I am able to sit down with young girls who are fatherless and can't understand why their fathers don't want to spend time with them. I am able to talk with that military spouse who can't wrap her mind around why she has to always be the one raising the kids by herself. I can help her when she's crying and asking why she always has to be the one lonely and all by herself.

A lot of people who don't understand the military life will tell wives "you knew what you were getting yourself into". I have found that in a lot of cases some did not know what was coming, because some were not always taught what to expect as a military wife. So yes, even though I went through a lot of hard times and some I brought upon myself, God has still gifted me, built me up, and equipped me to be able to help in those areas. I had to come to the realization of that as well. My mind had gotten so accustomed to thinking negatively about myself that I forgot God can still use me. I think about the many people in the bible that didn't do right, but in the end God turned their trials, dirt, pain and ugly into Beauty.

Today as I look at my life, I am living my BEST LIFE. My husband and I are doing great with the help of the Lord. I have a daughter graduating with the class of 2018 and heading to the College her heart desires with a scholarship. My oldest son who has been gone from us for a year and a few months is returning home to be with his family. My two younger children are holding it down in school with honor roll. So just that little bit right there can make you say, "Lord I know you as a God of change! I know you as a God of healing! I know you as a God of peace!"

That is the reason we cannot walk away from our connection to life which is God. He also places the right people in our life to help connect us back to him when He sees us down in the pit. As I look back over my life I thank God for his grace and mercy over my life, my husband life, and my kids' lives. Now I can walk with my head lifted high, with no shame because I know my God has set me free, and delivered me from all sin, pain, shame, depression, lying, cheating, and addiction. Because I leaned on Jesus, and not my own understanding in the time of hardship. So now my husband and I can live the life called BLESSED!

"He lifted me out of the pit of despair, out of the mud and the mire. He set my feet on solid ground and steadied me as I walked along." -Psalms 40:2

The Solution to the Struggles of Life

Rejection: In life we will face rejection, but as I have grown older, I have learned that God will allow some people to reject you for your protection. Sometimes he needs you to be rejected in order for you to depend on Him. I encourage you to not always look at rejection as a bad thing, because you will be able to go from rejection to rejoicing!

- *God's way is perfect. All the Lord's promises prove true. He is a shield for all who look to him for protection.* **2 Samuel-22:31**

Abuse: Our God is a God of Love, not harm or danger. He was placed on this earth to love and to be loved. He is a God of love! He will never leave us, never make us beg for His attention, and He will never abuse us. So why do we think He will put someone in our life to mistreat us, and abuse us?

- Nothing Can Separate **Us** from **God's Love** *What shall we say about such wonderful things as these? If God is for us, who can ever be against us?* **Romans 8:31**

**Depression:** When you are in a depressed state of mind, the enemy has a hold over you. But it's a hold that God can remove from over you if you allow Him to. Depression is a dark place and will make you feel as if you are by yourself, or just crazy. But I encourage you to keep your mind covered in the blood of Jesus and let Him renew your mind daily.

- *He lifted me out of the pit of despair, out of the mud and the mire. He set my feet on solid ground and steadied me as I walked along.* **Psalms 40:2**

- *When doubts filled my mind, your comfort gave me renewed hope and cheer.* **Psalms 94:19**

- *Don't copy the behavior and customs of this world, but let God transform you*

From Brokenness to Wholeness

into a new person by changing the way you think. Then you will learn to know God's will for you, which is good and pleasing and perfect. **Roman 12:2**

Addictions: An addiction is another spirit that the enemy has placed over you, and a Spirit that's never too big for God. The reason why most people are addicted to a drug, sex, gambling, lying, cheating, eating, etc. for such a long period of time is because THEY choose to stay addicted. It's a stronghold that only God can remove, but you must want to be delivered from that addiction. As long as you entertain that addiction, that's how long it will stay with you. Are you ready to be delivered on today?

- *The temptations in your life are no different from what others experience. And God is*

99

faithful. He will not allow the temptation to be more than you can stand. When you are tempted, he will show you a way out so that you can endure. **1 Corinthians 10:13**

Acknowledgments

As I began to write this book, my emotions were all over the place. I prayed a lot as I began to write. I thought about all the people who would come across my book, and I prayed that God would allow it to be read and received in love. I am very thankful for every one of you who has taken the time to invest in me, and taken the time to invest in yourself by purchasing this book. I pray you can pull something positive and encouraging from this reading.

A special thanks to my husband and children! Thank you all for pushing me, and loving me through the process. Thank you for accepting me for who I am in the Lord, and for accepting the many days I have dedicated my time to this book. I love you with all of my being and pray God gives every one of you, your heart's desire.

I thank my mom, and my sisters Ramona and Marlo. Thank you all so much for staying in my corner, praying for me and pushing me. Special thanks to my sister Melody, my prayer warrior, biggest supporter, and pusher. This woman has been calling me as God sees me for a long time now. I thank you for seeing what God has placed in me.

Pastor Sherry and Elder Gregory Ferrell, thank you for being who God has called you all to be. Thank you for prayers, teaching, and nurturing. I know being pastors can be tough sometimes, especially when working with a girl named Nadeen....LOL! I thank you all for your dedication to God first and to the church family second.

Thank you to all of my readers!!! I pray God touches you through this reading. I encourage you to look to God when you are facing a battle in life that's too hard for you. Always remember, NOTHING is EVER too hard for GOD!

www.ingramcontent.com/pod-product-compliance
Lightning Source LLC
Chambersburg PA
CBHW030148070426
42446CB00007BB/744